TRANSPORTATION EXPLORER

Can Airplanes Ski?

QUESTIONS AND ANSWERS ABOUT FLYING VEHICLES

by Heather E. Schwartz

PEBBLE
a capstone imprint

Published by Capstone Press, an imprint of Capstone
1710 Roe Crest Drive, North Mankato, Minnesota 56003
capstonepub.com

Library of Congress Cataloging-in-Publication Data is available on the Library of Congress website.
ISBN: 9780756582920 (hardcover)
ISBN: 9780756582876 (paperback)
ISBN: 9780756582883 (ebook PDF)

Summary: Jets, helicopters, and hot air balloons—an amazing variety of vehicles soar through the sky! How do they work, and where can they take us? Kids will find the answers to all their questions about vehicles that fly in this fun, interactive book.

Editorial Credits
Editor: Christopher Harbo; Designer: Terri Poburka; Media Researcher: Svetlana Zhurkin; Production Specialist: Katy LaVigne

Image Credits
Capstone Studio: Karon Dubke, 30; Dreamstime: Belinda Wu, 15 (airplane interior); Getty Images: Daniel Grill, 23 (boy), Digital Vision, 12, Hulton Archive, 32 (bottom), Jason Edwards, 20 (bottom), 31 (bottom), Nnehring, 8 (bottom), OzGraffiti, 26 (bottom), Rawpixel, 13 (cruise ship); Library of Congress: 6, 31 (top); NASA: JPL-Caltech, cover (bottom right), 18 (bottom), JPL-Caltech/ASU, 31 (middle), JPL-Caltech/ASU/MSSS, 18 (top), Ken Ulbrich, 28 (top); Newscom: ZUMA Press/Gene Blevins, 28 (bottom); Shutterstock: 23q (hello), AboutLife, 21 (girl), AerialVision_it, 10, Anatoly Foto, 25 (notepad), Andrii_Malysh, 9 (banner), annet999, cover (skis), Aphelleon, 17 (back), ASDF_Media, 9 (people), Backgroundy, 4 (bottom), badahos, 23 (airplane), blueeyes, cover (bottom middle), BOXX3D Design, 5 (back), djgis, cover (back), Dushlik, cover (airplane), Elenamiv, 7 (back), Eric Buermeyer, 9 (airplane), FooTToo, 14, FrameAngel, 15 (curtains), frantic00, cover (ski poles), Ground Picture, 29 (girl), HealthyCapture Studio, 25 (back), IM_photo, 3 (top), Jimmoyht, 25 (airplane), John k studio, 13 (airplane wings), John Lindsay-Smith, 32 (top), Jonathan Wilker, 26 (top), Karl R. Martin, 22 (left), Knumina Studios, 3 (middle right), Kobby Dagan, 22 (right), KonstantinChristian, 5 (bottom right), Love Silhouette, 3 (bottom right), Maria Martyshova (background), back cover and throughout, Michal Hudak, 3 (bottom left), Mr Doomits, 17 (helicopter), MrGarry, 19 (skis), Mykola Mazuryk, 17 (spiral lines), Natalya Timofeeva, 4 (back), Naypong Studio, 21 (back), Nerthuz, 19 (airplane), New Africa, 25 (pencil), photoschmidt, 24, polarbearstudio, 19 (back), Rocksweeper, cover (bottom left), Roman Sigaev, 13 (back), Ryan Fletcher, 8 (top), siraphat, 32 (middle), Standret, 11, Sunshine Seeds, 16, Tatiana Shepeleva, 11 (steering wheel), tovovan, 29 (back), Triff, 27 (space), Vadim Ovchinnikov, 15 (bedroom), Vector_Artist, 7 (airplane), Veniamin Kraskov, 4 (top), webreg30380, 9 (speech bubbles), Weenee, 27 (biplane); Svetlana Zhurkin: 3 (middle left); U.S. Navy: Senior Chief Mass Communication Specialist RJ Stratchko, 20 (top)

Printed and bound in China. 5834

Flying vehicles are all around us! Jumbo jets carry passengers to faraway places. Rescue helicopters rush to help people in danger. Military jets whoosh across the sky.

Let's learn more about flying vehicles. Read each question and try to guess the answer. Then turn the page to find out if you got it right!

How long was the first flight on a plane?

Brothers Orville and Wilbur Wright built the world's first powered plane. On December 17, 1903, Orville successfully flew the plane for the first time. His flight lasted only 12 seconds, and he traveled just 120 feet (36.6 meters).

Can an airplane fly upside down?

Stunt planes can fly upside down! Their wings are designed for upside-down flying. They also have powerful engines to make quick movements. Stunt planes can fly in loops, rolls, and spins.

Can an aircraft fly backward?

Helicopters can fly backward. They can also take off and land by moving straight up and down. These abilities make helicopters perfect for rescue missions. They can work in hard-to-reach places, such as rugged mountains and stormy seas.

Do passenger planes have steering wheels?

Passenger planes have many instruments for steering. A tiller turns the plane's front wheel when it's on the ground. In the air, a control wheel and pedals turn the plane. The control wheel adjusts fins on the wings. Pedals on the cockpit floor move the plane's rear rudder.

How can a ship fly?

A ship can fly when it has a balloon on board! An airship has a huge bag of air attached. The bag is filled with helium. This gas is lighter than air. With enough helium, the airship floats up into the sky.

Do passenger jets have secret rooms?

Shhh! Don't tell, but . . . some passenger jets *do* have a secret bedroom for the flight crew. The door for the room looks like a bathroom door. Behind it, a staircase leads to two rows of beds.

Can helicopters fly on other planets?

Yes! A tiny helicopter has flown on Mars. In 2021, NASA's Ingenuity Mars Helicopter arrived on the planet. The helicopter made 72 flights on Mars. It took pictures of the planet's surface.

Can airplanes ski?

In a sense, some planes *can* ski! Skibirds have skis on their landing gear. The skis allow the planes to safely land on snow and ice. Skibirds are perfect for carrying people and cargo to snowy places like Antarctica.

Could a balloon carry you into the sky?

A hot air balloon can send you soaring! It uses a burner to heat air. Since hot air is lighter than cool air, the balloon rises into the sky. Most hot air balloons can lift about 1,000 pounds (454 kilograms)!

Can you hold a flying vehicle in your hand?

Yes! Recreational drones are small enough to fit in your hand! They are flown by remote control. These drones can take photos and videos, race through the sky, and even perform in light shows!

Can planes write messages?

Skywriting planes create messages in the sky. Their pilots release a mixture of oil and smoke to form letters as they fly. The letters are huge so people on the ground can read them. Each letter can measure up to 1 mile (1.6 kilometers) long!

Can a plane fly into space?

Dream Chaser

Yes! Spaceplanes have rockets to blast into space. Some spaceplanes launch from the ground. Others are carried into the air by another aircraft. Then they launch in mid-flight. Dream Chaser and SpaceShipTwo are two types of spaceplanes.

SpaceShipTwo

What flying vehicle can you make by yourself?

A paper airplane is a flying vehicle you can make by yourself. Find a sheet of paper and follow these instructions to make your own!

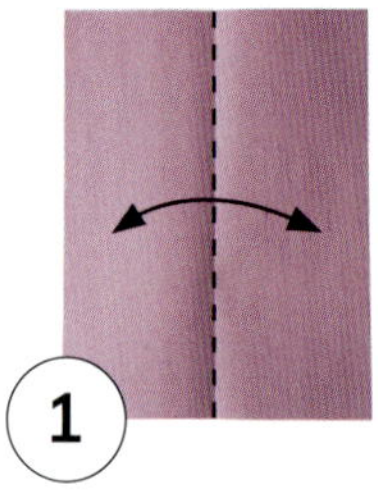

1. Fold the paper in half and unfold.

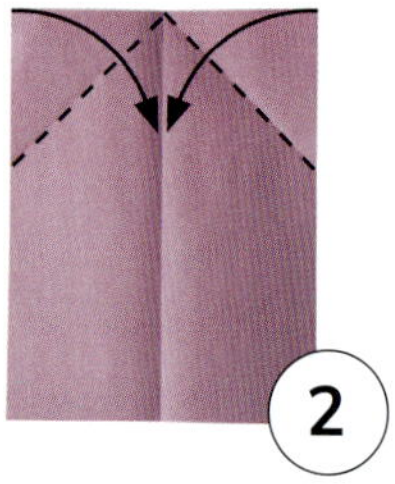

2. Fold the top corners to the center.

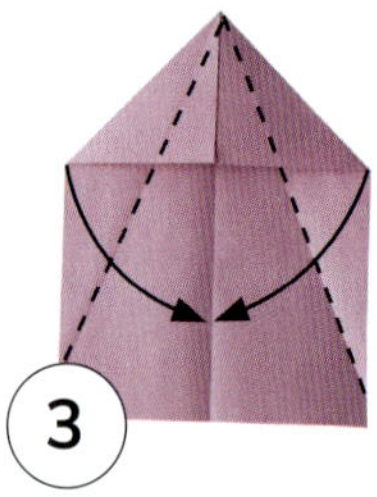

3. Fold the edges to the center.

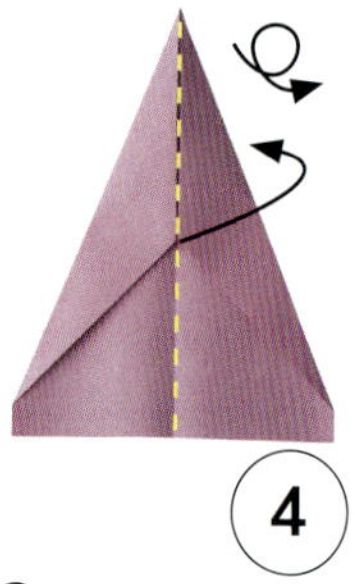

4. Fold the right side behind the left and rotate.

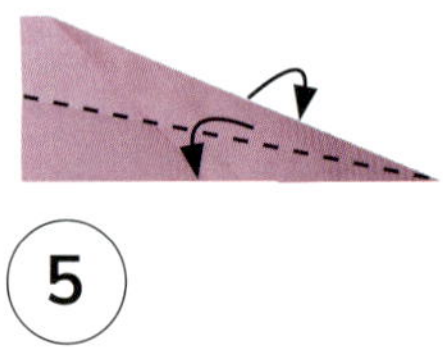

5. Fold the top layer even with the bottom edge. Repeat behind.

6. Lift the wings.

7. Fly your finished paper airplane!

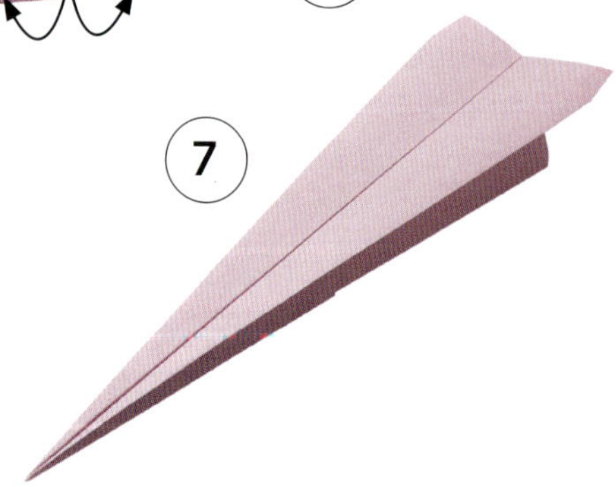

FUN FLYING VEHICLE FACTS!

Brothers Orville (right) and Wilbur Wright invented the first powered airplane in 1903. They started working on their idea when Orville was 7 and Wilbur was 11.

The NASA Ingenuity Mars Helicopter was solar powered. When it got low on power, it used sunlight to recharge on its own.

The LC-130 Hercules Skibird weighs 90,000 pounds (40,823 kg). That's equal to the weight of about seven male African elephants!

The huge Boeing 747 is made of six million parts. Half of them are fasteners such as nuts and bolts.

Airplane tires are made so they won't pop when the plane lands. They can land safely more than 500 times before needing service.

The first hot air balloon meant to carry a person was invented in 1783. It was tested by sending a sheep, a duck, and a rooster on a short flight.